• Puff paint applied with a stiff brush

These ideas books are *'just'* that. Ideas and methodologies to get your creative juices flowing. There is an assumption that you will adhere to simple safety guidelines. Also that readers have some basic knowledge of free-machine/motion work. The instructions are general in nature and open to wider interpretation. I give you permission to play with these and have fun!

You will need a basic level of equipment: heat gun, heat resistant surface (hot sheet), sewing machine (for some techniques) scissors, pokey tool, brushes etc… and, of course, Puff Paint!

Puff Paint: A Heat-Activ

How to apply Puff Paint.

Puff Paint can be applied in numerous ways to create different surface textures.

Several thin layers heated after each application will give a very dense, finely dappled surface. Marks made by the applicator will be evident.

A single thick layer heated, allowed to rest and heated again and repeated until maximum rise is achieved, will give a high pebbled texture. Again the marks of the applicator will be apparent.

Puff Paint can be blended – black and white can be mixed to give a grey scale, or simply marbled together.

Application can be made with your fingers, dab, swirl, smear (but wash your hands afterwards).

A soft paint brush will allow you to drip and use a dragging action with the Puff Paint. Make sure you do not overload the brush for this technique.

A stiff painting brush, using a flat brush, again place and drag (see front cover). Using only a little Puff Paint, grained lines can be formed. A round brush can be used in a stippling manner.

Foam applicators: different densities of foam will allow for 'cellular' marks to be made (natural sponge/foam). With a denser foam, peaked textures can be created.

Important. *All tools should be cleaned immediately after use. Dried Puff Paint is very difficult to remove.*

How to Cure Puff Paint, or, Making It Do Its Thing!

By allowing the Puff Paint to dry before heating, a lesser rise occurs.

Using a heat gun, heat by gently moving the gun across the area to which the Puff Paint been applied. Work over the surface rather than concentrating on one area at a time.

If you wish to maximise the rise, then heat and allow to cool, rest, heat and repeat. In that way the maximum amount of height is achieved.

Different types of Puff Paints are available in several from different manufacturers. Although each creates a dimentional effect, suitable for its designed purpose, not all are suitable for the more creative textile uses described in this book.

Throughout the book, only Craftynotions' black and white Puff Paint has been used.

• See Encrustations

Acrylic Paints. These can be applied either neat or watered down. With acrylics, other things may be added to make it easier to work the paint into the knobbly surface that has been created using Puff Paint. A small amount of acrylic matte medium could be added to improve flow of the acrylic, without interfering with the intensity of colour.

If a dark colour is put onto the surface of white Puff Paint (or a light colour onto black Puff Paint), and quickly wiped off with a soft cloth, an antiqued effect can be created. Then other colours can be layered up onto that surface.

Textile Paints. There are a number of different types of textile paint available. Those that have a thick consistency can be used in the same manner as acrylic paints. Those that are thinner, offer a more translucent application of colour that can be sequentially layered, or used as a ground for other colour application.

1. Antique Effect   2. Acrylic Paint   3. Craftynotions Creative Glaze   4. Versa Magic   5. Brilliance Ink

Transfer Paints (Disperse Dyes). These are intense colours that are normally used to create images on synthetic material. If painted directly onto Puff Paint after it has been activated, or on a sequence of heat applications, a rich painterly effect can be obtained.

Craftynotions Creative Colour Sprays. These can be sprayed after activation or after a series of heat applications. They provide a shimmering light-laden lustre and a rich application of colour *(See Encrustation)*

Gilding Creams, rub on gilding waxes and shoe polish. These products are ideal for enhancing the relief of the surface. Only the tiniest amount will visually lift the textures. Too much will be less effective.

Acrylic Wax. Apply over the surface, or add a little acrylic paint to create a colour glaze. This is best used when only the lightest of colour application is required.

Creative Colour Glazes. These offer a wet look to the puffed surface.

Stamping Pads. There are a myriad of types of ink pads

- Brilliance Inks offer a pearlescent lustre
- VersaMagic gives a matte flat colour
- VersaCraft are strong intense colours that can also be used on fabric
- Stazon, produces a strong multi-surface ink is another good one to try

These can be applied directly, or by using a transfer tool (eg Fantastix), or a small section of foam (eg Cut'n'Dry or make-up sponges) or a soft brush. You may need an extra application of heat from the heat gun to fix the ink.

All these techniques are for creative contemporary textile uses and can be used in combination. Although Puff Paint can be washed, these methods may not be compatible with washing.

(Background) Transfer paint

Elemental

You may need:

- A variety of applicators
- Cotton or heat resilient fabric for background

1. Brush Mark & Transfer Paint   2. Acrylic Paint   3. Beads   4. Gold Elemental Surface

Surfaces

Method:

- Apply a thin layer of Puff Paint over your chosen background with a stiff brush (see How To Apply Puff Paint for other suggestions).

- Activate with heat gun (remember if you let it dry before activating then you will get a smaller response to the puffing than if it is done when wet). This surface results in a suede-like feel and can be over-coloured with numerous colouring mediums. This is ideal for a background in its own right or cutting for strip bead-making. The advantage being that the thin application of Puff Paint selvedges the cut edge.

- By repeated overlays of a thin application of black or white Puff Paint, a very sophisticated surface can be created. Each layer may be coloured.

- By using different applicators, different marks can be delivered into the surface.

Some Further Possibilities.

- Cut strips from your newly created fabric and weave them

- Cut strips, or other shapes. Roll and either glue, or stitch the end down to create beads.

- Further adorn with threads, wires and glass beads

- Cut discs in several different sizes and stitch together with a spacer (eg felt washer) between layers. The edges can be painted with Puff Paint too

Encrustacians

You may need:

- Spatula or card applicator
- Cotton fabric for background
- A selection of Rainbow Drops, Mica-Flakes, jewelled squares
- You may also consider small pebbles, shells, glass beads etc.

Method:

- Apply a generous amount of Puff Paint to your surface. Embed your encrustaceans into the surface of the wet Puff Paint.

- Gently heat the surface until the shine disappears, or allow to dry.

- Activate the Puff Paint to create a rise, allow to cool for a few moments. Repeat once or twice as required until the

1. Jewelled Squares   2. Mica-Flakes   3. Rainbow Drops   4. Jewelled Squares

(Aren't they snails?)

puffing action no longer occurs (this repeated heating and cooling allows the Puff Paint to be fully cured as well as grabbing whatever embedded items you have used.

• Allow to cool. This newly created encrusted surface can be sprayed with Colour Sprays, painted, etc.

• Be aware if you wish to machine stitch this surface, you will need to consider the items that you embed, as they may not be suitable for use with machine embroidery. If you have put small pebbles on your piece then your needle will break! I personally find that this encrusted surface is much better further adorned with hand stitchery.

4.

Printing

You may need:

- Wooden printing blocks
- Karantha Spiral Texture Mat or similar unmounted rubber stamps with an open design
- Background material, either plain or previously coloured and/or stitched
- Applicators – brush or foam pad
- Textile paints
- Craftynotions Creative Colour Sprays
- Gilding creams and/or rub-on gilding waxes

1. Karantha Spiral Stamp   2. Karantha Spiral Stamp   3. Indian Print Block

Apply Puff Paint – black or white – to your stamp with either brush or foam brush applicator. Stamp it onto your chosen background fabric. Don't use too much Puff Paint as it will obscure the definition of the printed image. A little practice will enable you to control your results

- If you find that the Puff Paint, when heated, spreads sideways and reduces the definition of your print, try allowing the Puff Paint to air-dry for 10-20 minutes before heating. This will reduce the spread. If you allow the Puff Paint to dry completely, it will also reduce the rise

- When the Puff Paint print has been puffed, you may choose to overpaint with textile paints

or spray over with Colour Sprays. When these are dry you can further adorn the raised or background surface with gilding creams or lightly applied accent colour

Some Further Possibilities.

- Puff Paint on plain white cotton background puffed and sprayed with Colour Sprays

- Heavily free motion/machine stitchery background with Puff Paint applied and overpainted with textile paint

- Silk paper background previously gilded, printed Puff Paint with Spray and paint application and then further stitchery added after

Lacework

You may need:

- CraftMistress Romeo water soluble film
- Cotton machine thread
- Sewing machine

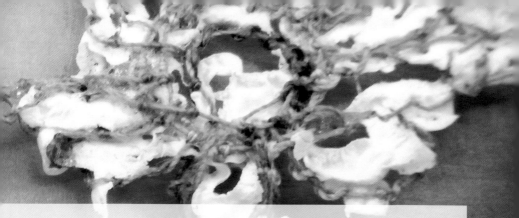

Method

- Place the Romeo on your heat resistant sheet (although the Puff Paint does not dissipate the Romeo, you will have to work quickly as prolonged exposure will allow the Puff Paint to seep through the Romeo

- Place the Puff Paint onto Romeo water soluble film

- Quickly add threads or slivers of light weight fabric. Heat the Puff Paint following guidelines. Do not be alarmed if the Romeo film buckles. This is a reaction to the heat, and will not affect the usability of the Romeo or the Puff Paint

- When the Puff Paint is fully cured and cool, it may be stitched (if the Puff Paint is not fully cured or allowed to dry, when it is pierced with the machine needle it might ooze, so it is important that it is fully cured or allowed to dry, if you are uncertain, overnight, before stitching

- Either using free motion/ machine embroidery or conventional stitch patterns, stitch over the Puff/water soluble combination. The stitch pattern should be open and lacey to avoid obscuring the puffed surface

- Dissolve away Romeo in copious amounts of water. When all the Romeo has been dissolved away, allow your piece to dry thoroughly

- Paint/spray Puff Paint to suit

This newly formed fabric can be used as a background or as an art work in its own right. It may be further adorned with hand stitching, beadery etc.

Trapping a

1.

2.

3.

You may need:

- Suitable background material
- Cotton, linen or silk threads

Method

- Create some circles with Puff Paint on a suitable background. Lay into the wet Puff Paint heat resistant threads. You may like to try different types of thread, ribbons, knitted constructions, tapes, thick or thin. Also consider the scale of your work.

- You could lay your threads in a wheel formation, or randomly radiating the outer edge, or just spanning the outline to give a fringed effect.

- Press threads into wet Puff Paint with a pokey tool.

1. Concentric Circles   2. Linear Pattern   3. Circular Fringing

d Layering

- If you are not going to use any colouring on the Puff Paint, then the choice of only using black or white threads can be very creative as well as giving a powerful statement.

- With all these considerations, when you have made your choice, use the heat gun to puff the Puff Paint!

- You may have to poke some threads into the expanding medium as you heat it. Try a wooden skewer (as it won't transmit heat), or use an appropriately insulated pokey tool.

- *Remember,* if you let the Puff Paint dry, it won't rise as much when heated. This may be of advantage in this particular method of use as, by repeating the process over the activated

surface, a layered effect can be achieved (you may need to be patient and allow the time to do this).

Some Further Possibilities.

- As you add layers, the threads that you choose can be the same, or different colours, thicknesses etc. Overlaying them in different manners, can achieve a richly layer surface

- Try different shapes (singular, multiple or concentric) squares, lines or abstract. Also concentric shapes. By adding hand stitchery, or looking at wrapping areas to constrict the threads, some elaborate constructions can be made.

- This is a very effective decorative process, but it does require a little patience!

• Encrustation with Glitter Squares

Suppliers

Most supplies used within this book are available from Craftynotions
(www.craftynotions.com) and Craftynotions' stockists.
For further information visit www.karanthapublishing.com

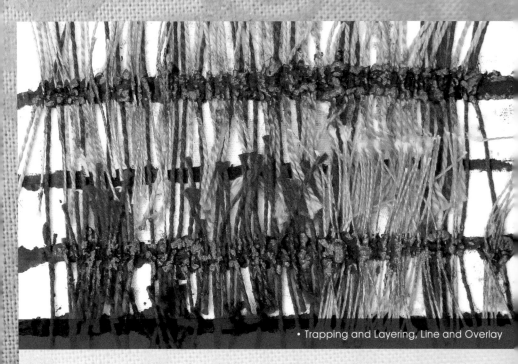

• Trapping and Layering, Line and Overlay

In the same series
It's Just... Rusty Stuff (Karantha Publishing)

Also by Sarah Lawrence
Wild Women, 20 to Make (Search Press)

Art Dolls, 20 to Make (Search Press)

Silk Paper for Textile Artists (A&C Black)

And on DVD
Simply Fused (Rare Bird)

The Decorated Surface (Rare Bird)

Acknowlegements
Thanks to Peggy, Adam, Christine W, Fran, David
and of course my friend Christine

Designed & printed with vegetable inks on pulp sourced from sustainable forests by www.newark-printing.com

9 780956 323101

KITTIWAKE

WALKS AROUND

LUDLOW

& MORTIMER COUNTRY

Les Lumsdon and Peta & Phil Sams

Twenty Great Walks

KITTIWAKE

Walks guides which detail superb routes
in most parts of Wales & the Borders.

From Anglesey and Snowdonia to the Brecon Beacons,
and from Machynlleth and Welshpool to Pembrokeshire and the Llŷn
including Gower and the Borders, they offer a range of
carefully researched routes with something for all abilities.

Each guide has been compiled and written by
dedicated authors who really know their particular area.

They are all presented in the **KITTIWAKE**
clear and easy-to-use style

For latest details of the expanding range visit:

www.kittiwake-books.com

KITTIWAKE
3 Glantwymyn Village Workshops
Glantwymyn, Machynlleth
Montgomeryshire SY20 8LY